A HANDBOOK OF EU VAT LEGISLATION

A HANDBOOK OF EU VAT LEGISLATION

Rita de la Feria

University of Dublin, Trinity College

KLUWER LAW
INTERNATIONAL

Published by:
Kluwer Law International
P.O. Box 85889
2508 CN The Hague
The Netherlands
E-mail: sales@kluwerlaw.com
Website: http://www.kluwerlaw.com

Sold and distributed in North, Central and South America by:
Aspen Publishers, Inc.
7201 McKinney Circle
Frederick, MD 21704
USA
E-mail: customer.care@aspenpubl.com

Sold and distributed in all other countries by:
Extenza-Turpin Distribution Services
Stratton Business Park
Pegasus Drive
Biggleswade
Bedfordshire SG18 8QB
United Kingdom
E-mail: sales@kluwerlaw.com

Printed on acid-free paper

ISBN 90-411-2242-7
© 2004 Kluwer Law International

Printed in The Netherlands.

To my grandfather and mentor
Dr. Ramon Machado de la Feria

Introduction

The aim of this publication is to provide, for the first time, a compilation of all EU VAT legislation to date.

Whilst compilations of VAT law exist in most Member States, these focus primarily upon the VAT law of the particular country, citing only the most essential EU VAT legislation. Consequently, these compilations have tended to concentrate upon domestic provisions, providing only a referential treatment of EU VAT legislation.

This publication proposes to consider VAT law from a different perspective, *i.e.*, from an EU perspective: considering EU VAT legislation not as a reference but as ultimately the source of all domestic VAT legislation.

As the English language progressively becomes the international language of business, it is appropriate that this publication should be presented in this language, the sole exception being those cases where an English language official version of the relevant legislative instrument is not available. Where this has happened, the legislation is presented in the French language, as indicated in the 'contents' section of the publication. The same principle applies to the European Court of Justice case-law.

However, in order to facilitate understanding of the EU VAT terminology, the publication contains, at the end, a translation table of the most frequently used VAT terms in all current languages of the European Union.

With a view to facilitating consultation of the legal provisions and also to provide the reader with a systematic perception of the EU VAT system, this publication has been divided into four parts, as follows:

    I. EU Common System of VAT – Basis of Assessment;
   II. VAT Refund System for Taxable Persons Not Established in the Territory of the Country;
 III. Statistical System for Statistics on Trade of Goods between Member States – Intrastat;
 IV. Administrative Cooperation & Mutual Assistance (Including VIES and FISCALIS).

These sections represent four, out of the five, principal areas in which EU VAT legislation has been approved.[1]

---

[1] The fifth area of legislation concerns VAT as one of the Community's own resources. The legislation regarding this aspect of EU VAT will not be included in this compilation, as the spectrum of its

Each of these sections has then been subdivided into the following three subsections:

A. Legislation in force
B. Legislation no longer in force
C. Legislation in preparation

The purpose of including legislation no longer in force and legislation in preparation within this publication is to provide a view of both the past and the possible future workings of the EU VAT system.[2] The past can be relevant in the analysis of particular cases that took place prior to the present legislation coming into force. The proposals can be relevant insofar as they allow a detailed study of the potential legislation before it comes into force and may act as ancillary to the interpretation of the present legislation.

Each subsection includes the legislation approved in that area. Where this legislation has been amended, the version presented will *always* be the consolidated version. Amendments and derogations, where they exist, as well as any implementing and ancillary legislation, will also be included.

All legislation in force has been footnoted and cross-referenced. In the case of the Sixth Directive, the primary community legislation in force in the area of VAT, this has been done on an Article-by-Article basis. The notes make reference to, amongst others, the following aspects:

– Amendments introduced to the legislation since it came into force;
– Proposals presented by the Commission for amending or substituting legislation in force;
– Authorisations granted to the various Member States to introduce derogation measures;
– Authorisations granted to the various Member States to introduce derogation measures which have ceased to have effect;
– Proposals presented by the Commission regarding derogation measures;
– Ancillary legislation in force;
– Ancillary legislation which has ceased to have effect;
– Connected legislation in force;
– Connected legislation no longer in force;
– European Court of Justice VAT cases.

---

influence is limited to EU budgetary concerns. Details of the legislation approved in this area, however, can be found in the legislation index, at the end of the publication.
[2] Please note than for the purposes of this publication 'legislation no longer in force' is taken as meaning legislation which has ceased to have effect as regards VAT. Thus, in certain cases the legislation included under this heading might still be in force insofar as other subjects are concerned.

In the end of the publication tables have been included documenting as follows:

A. *Legislation index* – all EU VAT legislation arranged in chronological order;

B. *EU VAT cases tables* – two tables European Court of Justice's VAT Cases. The first is an index arranged on case number basis; the second arranges the judgments by the European Court Justice based on the legislative provisions upon which they focus;

C. *VAT rates tables* – details of the VAT rates applicable in all Member States as well as a table detailing the VAT rates applicable to selected goods and services in all Member States;

D. *Translation table* – as above, this table contains the main VAT terms translated into all languages of the European Union;

E. Web-sites index – list of web-sites containing information on the EU VAT system or the domestic VAT systems of the Member States. Indication of the languages in which the site is available, is also provided.

All information included, namely the legislation and the European Court of Justice's cases, is current up to 31 March 2005.

This publication will be updated through supplements on a bi-annual basis.

TITLE X – EXEMPTIONS

Article 13

Exemptions within the territory of the country

A. Exemptions for certain activities in the public interest

1. Without prejudice to other Community provisions, Member States shall exempt the following under conditions which they shall lay down for the purpose of ensuring the correct and straightforward application of such exemptions and of preventing any possible evasion, avoidance or abuse:

   (a) the supply by the public postal services of services other than passenger transport and telecommunications services, and the supply of goods incidental thereto;

   (b) hospital and medical care and closely related activities undertaken by bodies governed by public law or, under social conditions comparable to those applicable to bodies governed by public law, by hospitals, centers for medical treatment or diagnosis and other duly recognized establishments of a similar nature;

   (c) the provision of medical care in the exercise of the medical and paramedical professions as defined by the Member State concerned;

   (d) supplies of human organs, blood and milk;

   (e) services supplied by dental technicians in their professional capacity and dental prostheses supplied by dentists and dental technicians;

   (f) services supplied by independent groups of persons whose activities are exempt from or are not subject to value added tax, for the purpose of rendering their members the services directly necessary for the exercise of their activity, where these groups merely claim from their members exact reimbursement of their share of the joint expenses, provided that such exemption is not likely to produce distortion of competition;

   (g) the supply of services and of goods closely linked to welfare and social security work, including those supplied by old people's homes, by bodies governed by public law or by other organizations recognized as charitable by the Member State concerned;

   (h) the supply of services and of goods closely linked to the protection of children and young persons by bodies governed by public law or by other organizations recognized as charitable by the Member State concerned;

   (i) children's or young people's education, school or university education, vocational training or retraining, including the supply of services and of goods closely related thereto, provided by bodies governed by public law having such as their aim or by other organizations defined by the Member State concerned as having similar objects;

(j) tuition given privately by teachers and covering school or university education;

(k) certain supplies of staff by religious or philosophical institutions for the purpose of subparagraphs (b), (g), (h) and (i) of this Article and with a view to spiritual welfare;

(l) supply of services and goods closely linked thereto for the benefit of their members in return for a subscription fixed in accordance with their rules by non-profit-making organizations with aims of a political, trade union, religious, patriotic, philosophical, philanthropic or civic nature, provided that this exemption is not likely to cause distortion of competition;

(m) certain services closely linked to sport or physical education supplied by non-profit-making organizations to persons taking part in sport or physical education;

(n) certain cultural services and goods closely linked thereto supplied by bodies governed by public law or by other cultural bodies recognized by the Member State concerned;

(o) the supply of services and goods by organizations whose activities are exempt under the provisions of subparagraphs (b), (g), (h), (i), (l), (m) and (n) above in connection with fund-raising events organized exclusively for their own benefit provided that exemption is not likely to cause distortion of competition. Member States may introduce any necessary restrictions in particular as regards the number of events or the amount of receipts which give entitlement to exemption;

(p) the supply of transport services for sick or injured persons in vehicles specially designed for the purpose by duly authorized bodies;

(q) activities of public radio and television bodies other than those of a commercial nature.

2. (a) Member States may make the granting to bodies other than those governed by public law of each exemption provided for in (1)(b), (g), (h), (i), (l), (m) and (n) of this Article subject in each individual case to one or more of the following conditions: – they shall not systematically aim to make a profit, but any profits nevertheless arising shall not be distributed, but shall be assigned to the continuance or improvement of the services supplied,

– they shall be managed and administered on an essentially voluntary basis by persons who have no direct or indirect interest, either themselves or through intermediaries, in the results of the activities concerned,

- they shall charge prices approved by the public authorities or which do not exceed such approved prices or, in respect of those services not subject to approval, prices lower than those charged for similar services by commercial enterprises subject to value added tax,

- exemption of the services concerned shall not be likely to create distortions of competition such as to place at a disadvantage commercial enterprises liable to value added tax.

(b) The supply of services or goods shall not be granted exemption as provided for in (1)(b), (g), (h), (i), (l), (m) and (n) above if:

- it is not essential to the transactions exempted,

- its basic purpose is to obtain additional income for the organization by carrying out transactions which are in direct competition with those of commercial enterprises liable for value added tax.

B. Other exemptions

Without prejudice to other Community provisions, Member States shall exempt the following under conditions which they shall lay down for the purpose of ensuring the correct and straightforward application of the exemptions and of preventing any possible evasion, avoidance or abuse:

(a) insurance and reinsurance transactions, including related services performed by insurance brokers and insurance agents;

(b) the leasing or letting of immovable property excluding:

1. the provision of accommodation, as defined in the laws of the Member States, in the hotel sector or in sectors with a similar function, including the provision of accommodation in holiday camps or on sites developed for use as camping sites;

2. the letting of premises and sites for parking vehicles;

3. lettings of permanently installed equipment and machinery;

4. hire of safes.

Member States may apply further exclusions to the scope of this exemption;

(c) supplies of goods used wholly for an activity exempted under this Article or under Article 28(3)(b) when these goods have not given rise to the right to deduction, or of goods on the acquisition or production of which, by virtue of Article 17(6), value added tax did not become deductible;

(d) the following transactions:

1. the granting and the negotiation of credit and the management of credit by the person granting it;

2. the negotiation of or any dealings in credit guarantees or any other security for money and the management of credit guarantees by the person who is granting the credit;

3. transactions, including negotiation, concerning deposit and current accounts, payments, transfers, debts, cheques and other negotiable instruments, but excluding debt collection and factoring;

4. transactions, including negotiation, concerning currency, bank notes and coins used as legal tender, with the exception of collectors' items; 'collectors' items' shall be taken to mean gold, silver or other metal coins or bank notes which are not normally used as legal tender or coins of numismatic interest;

5. transactions, including negotiation, excluding management and safekeeping, in shares, interests in companies or associations, debentures and other securities, excluding:

   – documents establishing title to goods,

   – the rights or securities referred to in Article 5(3);

6. management of special investment funds as defined by Member States;

(e) the supply at face value of postage stamps valid for use for postal services within the territory of the country, fiscal stamps, and other similar stamps;

(f) betting, lotteries and other forms of gambling, subject to conditions and limitations laid down by each Member State;

(g) the supply of buildings or parts thereof, and of the land on which they stand, other than as described in Article 4(3)(a);

(h) the supply of land which has not been built on other than building land as described in Article 4(3)(b).

C. Options

Member States may allow taxpayers a right of option for taxation in cases of:

(a) letting and leasing of immovable property;

(b) the transactions covered in B(d), (g) and (h) above.

Member States may restrict the scope of this right of option and shall fix the details of its use.

Notes

Amendments in preparation

– Article 399 of Proposal for a Council Directive on the common system of value added tax (Recast) – **COM(2004) 246 final, 15 April 2004** [I.C.2.a.(6).].

– Proposal for a Council Directive amending Directive 77/388/EEC as regards Value Added Tax on services provided in the postal sector – **COM(2003) 234 final, 5 May 2003 and COM(2004) 468 final, 8 July 2004** [I.C.1 .a.(3).].

Ancillary legislation in preparation

– Proposal for a Council Regulation laying down implementing measures for Directive 77/388/EEC on the common system of value added tax – **COM(2004)641 final/2, 25 October 2004** [I.C.2.c.(3)].

Connected legislation no longer in force

– Article 10 and Annex A(16), (17), (18) and (19) of the **Second Council Directive 67/228/EEC of 11 April 1967** [I.B.1.].

Connected legislation in preparation

– Articles 128, 129, 130, 131, 132, 133 and 134 of Proposal for a Council Directive on the common system of value added tax (Recast) – **COM(2004) 246 final, 15 April 2004** [I.C.2.a.(6).].

EU VAT cases

Postal services (paragraph A(1)(a))

Case 107/84   *Commission of the European Communities v Federal Republic of Germany*

By exempting from VAT the services provided by transport undertakings for the public postal services, Germany failed to fulfil its obligations under the EEC Treaty and under the provisions of Article 13A(1)(a) of the Sixth Directive.

Medical services (paragraph A(1)(b) and (c))

Case 353/85   *Commission of the European Communities v United Kingdom of Great Britain and Northern Ireland*

By exempting supplies of goods from the imposition of VAT, the United Kingdom failed to fulfil its obligations under Article 13A(1)(c) of the Sixth Directive.

Case 122/87   *Commission of the European Communities v Italian Republic*

By exempting from value-added tax the services provided by veterinary surgeons in the exercise of their profession, Italy failed to fulfil its obligations under Article 13A(1)(c) of the Sixth Directive.

C-216/97   *Jennifer Gregg and Mervyn Gregg v Commissioners of Customs and Excise*

Article 13A(1) of the Sixth Directive is to be interpreted as meaning that the terms 'other duly recognised establishments of a similar nature' and 'other organisations recognised as charitable by the Member State concerned', which appear in subparagraphs (b) and (g) of that provision respectively, do not exclude from that exemption natural persons running a business.

C-384/98   *D. v W.*

Article 13A(1)(c) of the Sixth Directive is to be interpreted as not applying to the provision of medical services which do not consist in providing medical care, by diagnosing and treating a disease or any other health disorder, but in establishing the genetic affinity of individuals through biological tests.

C-76/99   *Commission of the European Communities v French Republic*

By levying VAT on fixed allowances for the taking of samples for medical analysis, France failed to fulfil its obligations under Article 13A(1)(b) of the Sixth Directive.

C-141/00   *Ambulanter Pflegedienst Kugler GmbH v Finanzamt fur Korperschaften I in Berlin*

Out-care services provided by a limited company are regarded as exempt under Article 13A(1)(c) or (g) of the Sixth Directive.

C-45/01   *Christoph-Dornier-Stiftung Klinische Psychologie v Finanzamt Giessen*

1. Psychotherapeutic treatment given in an out-patient facility of a foundation governed by private law by qualified psychologists who are not doctors is not an activity closely related to hospital or medical care within the meaning of Article 13A(1)(b) of the Sixth Council Directive, except where such treatment is actually given as a service ancillary to the hospital or medical care received by the patients in question and constituting the principal service. However, the term medical care in that provision must be interpreted as covering all provision of medical care envisaged in letter (c) of the same provision, including services provided by persons who are not doctors but who give paramedical services, such as psychotherapeutic treatment given by qualified psychologists.

2. Recognition of an establishment for the purposes of Article 13A(1)(b) of the Sixth Directive 77/388 does not presuppose a formal recognition procedure; nor must such recognition necessarily derive from national tax law provisions. Where the national rules pertaining to recognition contain restrictions which exceed the limits of the discretion allowed to Member States under that provision, it is for the national court to determine, in the light of all the relevant facts, whether a taxable person must none the less be regarded as an other duly recognised establishment of a similar nature within the meaning of that provision.

3. Since the exemption envisaged in Article 13A(1)(c) of the Sixth Directive 77/388 is not dependent on the legal form of the taxable person providing the medical or paramedical services referred to in that provision, psychotherapeutic treatment provided by a foundation governed by private law and given by psychotherapists employed by the foundation may benefit from that exemption.

4. In circumstances such as those in the main proceedings, Article 13A(1)(b) and (c) of the Sixth Directive 77/388 may be relied on by a taxable person before a national court in order to contest the application of rules of national law which are incompatible with that provision.

C-212/01   *Margarete Unterpertinger v Pensionsversicherungsanstalt der Arbeiter*

Article 13A(1)(c) of Sixth Council Directive is to be interpreted as meaning that the exemption from value added tax under that provision does not apply to the services of a doctor consisting of making an expert report on a person's state of health in order to support or exclude a claim for payment of a disability pension. The fact that the medical expert was instructed by a court or pension insurance institution is irrelevant in that respect.

C-307/01   *Peter d'Ambrumenil, Dispute Resolution Services Ltd v Commissioners of Customs and Excise*

1. Article 13A(1)(c) of Sixth Council Directive, is to be interpreted as meaning that the exemption from VAT under that provision applies to medical services consisting of:

   – conducting medical examinations of individuals for employers or insurance companies,

   – the taking of blood or other bodily samples to test for the presence of viruses, infections or other diseases on behalf of employers or insurers, or

   – certification of medical fitness, for example, as to fitness to travel,

   where those services are intended principally to protect the health of the person concerned.

2. The said exemption does not apply to the following services, performed in the exercise of the medical profession:

   – giving certificates as to a person's medical condition for purposes such as entitlement to a war pension,

   – medical examinations conducted with a view to the preparation of an expert medical report regarding issues of liability and the quantification of damages for individuals contemplating personal injury litigation,

   – the preparation of medical reports following examinations referred to in the previous indent and medical reports based on medical notes without conducting a medical examination,

- medical examinations conducted with a view to the preparation of expert medical reports regarding professional medical negligence for individuals contemplating litigation,

- the preparation of medical reports following examinations referred to in the previous indent and medical reports based on medical notes without conducting a medical examination.

Independent groups of people (paragraph A(1)(f))

Case 348/87 *Stichting Litvoering Financiele Actiers v Staatssecretaris van Financien*

The transactions which must be exempted from turnover tax pursuant to Article 13(A)(1)(f) of the Sixth Directive, do not cover the activities of a foundation which consists exclusively in the organization and performance of work which is related to the activities of another foundation, against reimbursement of expenses actually incurred, where the other foundation acts as an umbrella organization for a number of bodies exercising an activity which is exempt or for which they are not taxable and, solely for those bodies, performs services as described in the aforesaid provision of the Sixth Directive.

C-8/01 *Assurandør-Societetet, acting on behalf of Taksatorringen v Skatteministeriet*

1. Article 13A(1)(f) of Sixth Council Directive 77/388 must be construed as meaning that the grant of exemption from value added tax under that provision to an association such as that in issue in the main proceedings and which satisfies all of the other conditions of that provision must be refused if there is a genuine risk that the exemption may by itself, immediately or in the future, give rise to distortions of competition.

2. National legislation which allows a temporary exemption to be granted where doubt exists as to whether that exemption, such as that in the case in the main proceedings, is liable at a later date to give rise to distortions of competition is compatible with Article 13A(1)(f) of Sixth Directive 77/388, provided that the exemption is renewed only for as long as the person concerned satisfies the conditions of that provision.

3. The fact that large insurance companies have the assessments of damage to motor vehicles carried out by their own experts, thereby avoiding liability for value added tax in respect of the provision of such services, is not such as to have any bearing on the answers to be given to the above questions.

Welfare and social security work services (paragraph A(1)(g))

C-453/93 *W. Bulthuis-Griffioen v Inspecteur der Omzetbelasting*

Article 13A(1)(g) of the Sixth Directive, is to be interpreted as meaning that a trader who is a natural person cannot claim exemption under this provision, which expressly reserves the exemption to bodies governed by public law or other organizations recognized as charitable by the Member State concerned.

C-216/97   *Jennifer Gregg and Mervyn Gregg v Commissioners of Customs and Excise*

Article 13A(1) of the Sixth Directive is to be interpreted as meaning that the terms 'other duly recognised establishments of a similar nature' and 'other organisations recognised as charitable by the Member State concerned', which appear in subparagraphs (b) and (g) of that provision respectively, do not exclude from that exemption natural persons running a business.

C-141/00   *Ambulanter Pflegedienst Kugler GmbH v Finanzamt fur Korperschaften I in Berlin*

Out-care services provided by a limited company are regarded as exempt under Article 13A(1)(c) or (g) of the Sixth Directive.

The exemption provided for in Article 13A(1)(g) of the Sixth Directive may be relied upon by a taxable person before national courts, i.e., it has direct effect.

C-498/03   *Kingscrest Associates Ltd and Montecello Ltd v Commissioners of Customs & Excise*

(1) In order to clarify the meaning of the expression "charitable" contained in Article 13A(1)(g) and (h) of Sixth Council Directive, reference must be made to the other language versions of those provisions, and the term cannot be given the meaning which it has in national law if that would lead to divergent interpretations.

(2) The fact that an economic operator who carries out operations treated as exempt by Article 13A(1)(g) and (h) of the Sixth Directive aims at making a profit does not in principle constitute an obstacle to its being regarded as a "charitable organisation".

(3) The Member States enjoy a discretion as to whether to grant a private entity, for the purposes of the abovementioned provisions, the status of a "charitable organisation", but, when exercising that discretion, they must observe the principle of neutrality of VAT and the principle of equal treatment as between taxable persons and must have regard to the nature of the activity and the aims for which it is carried on, so that it is classified by reference to predetermined, objective and abstract criteria which take account of the nature of the business, its organisational structure and the manner in which it is conducted. In all cases, it is for the national court to appraise the extent to which such limitations are complied with.

[*Opinion of the Advocate-General*]

Protection of children and young persons (paragraph A(1)(h))

C-498/03   *Kingscrest Associates Ltd and Montecello Ltd v Commissioners of Customs & Excise*

(1) In order to clarify the meaning of the expression "charitable" contained in Article 13A(1)(g) and (h) of Sixth Council Directive, reference must be made to the other language versions of those provisions, and the term cannot be given the meaning which it has in national law if that would lead to divergent interpretations.

(2) The fact that an economic operator who carries out operations treated as exempt by Article 13A(1)(g) and (h) of the Sixth Directive aims at making a profit does not in principle constitute an obstacle to its being regarded as a "charitable organisation".

(3) The Member States enjoy a discretion as to whether to grant a private entity, for the purposes of the abovementioned provisions, the status of a "charitable organisation", but, when exercising that discretion, they must observe the principle of neutrality of VAT and the principle of equal treatment as between taxable persons and must have regard to the nature of the activity and the aims for which it is carried on, so that it is classified by reference to predetermined, objective and abstract criteria which take account of the nature of the business, its organisational structure and the manner in which it is conducted. In all cases, it is for the national court to appraise the extent to which such limitations are complied with.

[*Opinion of the Advocate-General*]

Education services (paragraph A(1)(i))

C-287/00   *Commission of the European Communities v Federal Republic of Germany*

By exempting from VAT the research activities of public-sector higher-education establishments Germany failed to fulfil its obligations under Article 2 of the Sixth Directive.

Trade-unions (paragraph A(1)(l))

C-149/97   *The Institute of the Motor Industry v Commissioners of Customs and Excise*

It is for the national court to assess whether a voluntary association of persons working in the retail sector of the motor industry is a non-profit making organisation with aims of a trade-union nature within the meaning of Article 13A(1)(l) of the Sixth Directive.

Sport organisations (paragraph A(1)(m))

C-124/96   *Commission of the European Communities v Kingdom of Spain*

By providing that VAT exemption for services closely linked to sport or physical education applied only to private establishments whose membership fees did not exceed a specified amount, Spain failed to fulfil its obligations under Article 13A(1)(m) of the Sixth Directive.

C-150/99   *Stockholm Lindopark AB v Svenska Staten (Swedish State)*

Articles 13A(1)(m) and 13B(b) of the Sixth Directive preclude national legislation from providing for a general exemption from VAT for the supply of premises and other facilities and the related supply of accessories or other arrangements for the practice of sport or physical education, including services supplied by profit-making organisations.

The implementation of a general exemption from VAT for the supply of premises and other facilities and the related supply of accessories or other arrangements for the practice of sport or physical education, where no such general exemption is to be found in the Sixth Directive, constitutes a serious breach of Community law that can render a Member State liable in damages.

C-174/00   *Kennemer Golf & Country Club v Inspecteur Belastingdienst Particulieren/ Ondernemingen Haarlem*

The use of facilities of a golf club in return for payment of subscription fees must be regarded as an exempt supply of services exempt under Article 13A(1)(m) of the Sixth Directive.

Cultural services and goods (paragraph A(1)(n))

C-144/00   *Criminal proceedings against Matthias Hoffmann*

Article 13A(1)(n) of the Sixth Directive is to be interpreted to the effect that the expression 'other [recognised] cultural bodies' does not exclude soloists performing individually.

The heading of Article 13A of that directive does not, of itself, entail restrictions on the possibilities of exemption provided for by that provision.

Bodies managed on voluntary basis (second indent of paragraph A(2)(a))

C-267/00   *Commissioners of Customs and Excise v The Zoological Society of London*

Certain services carried out by a society in the administration of two zoological gardens must be considered exempt under the second indent of Article 13A(2)(a) of the Sixth Directive.

Insurance and reinsurance transactions (paragraph B(a))

C-349/96   *Card Protection Plan Ltd (CPP) v Commissioners of Customs and Excise*

Article 13B(a) of the Sixth Directive is to be interpreted as meaning that a taxable person, not being an insurer, who, in the context of a block policy of which he is the holder, procures for his customers, who are insured, insurance cover from an insurer who assumes the risk covered, performs an insurance transaction.

It is for the national court to determine what the appropriate criteria are for deciding, for VAT purposes, whether a transaction which comprises several elements is to be regarded as a single supply or as two or more distinct supplies to be assessed separately.

It is incompatible with Article 13B(a) of the Sixth Directive for a Member State to restrict the scope of the exemption for 'insurance ... transactions' to supplies made by persons permitted to carry on insurance business under the law of that Member State.

C-240/99   *Forsakringsaktiebolaget Skandia (publ)*

A commitment assumed by an insurance company to carry out, in return for remuneration at market rates, the activities of another insurance company, which is a 100% subsidiary and which would continue to conclude insurance contracts in its own name, does not constitute an insurance transaction within the meaning of Article 13B(a) of the Sixth Directive.

C-8/01   *Assurandør-Societetet, acting on behalf of Taksatorringen v Skatteministeriet*

1. Article 13B(a) of Sixth Council Directive must be construed as meaning that motor vehicle damage assessments carried out, on behalf of its members, by an association whose members are insurance companies are neither insurance transactions nor services related to insurance transactions that are performed by insurance brokers or insurance agents within the meaning of that provision.

2. The fact that large insurance companies have the assessments of damage to motor vehicles carried out by their own experts, thereby avoiding liability for value added tax in respect of the provision of such services, is not such as to have any bearing on the answers to be given to the above question.

C-308/01   *GIL Insurance Ltd, UK Consumer Electronics Ltd, Consumer Electronics Insurance Co. Ltd, Direct Vision Rentals Ltd, Homecare Insurance Ltd, Pinnacle Insurance plc v Commissioners of Customs and Excise*

Article 13(B)(a) of the Sixth Directive, under which insurance transactions are exempt from VAT, does not preclude, in the case of a tax on insurance premiums such as that at issue in the main proceedings, the introduction of a special rate which is identical to the standard rate of VAT, since that tax is compatible with Article 33 of the Sixth Directive, so that the procedure provided for in Article 27 of that directive, which obliges any Member State wishing to introduce special measures for derogation from that directive to seek prior authorisation from the Council of the European Union, does not have to be complied with before the introduction of that rate.

C-472/03   *Staatssecretaris van Financiën v Arthur Andersen & Co. Accountants c.s.*

Article 13B(a) of Sixth Council Directive must be interpreted as meaning that 'back office' activities, consisting in rendering services, for payment, to an insurance company do not constitute the performance of services relating to insurance transactions carried out by an insurance broker or an insurance agent within the meaning of that provision.

Letting of immovable property (paragraph B(b)and C(a))

Case 173/88   *Skatteministeriet v Morten Henriksen*

> Article 13B(b) of the Sixth Directive must be interpreted as meaning that the phrase 'premises and sites for parking vehicles' covers the letting of all places designed to be used for parking vehicles, including closed garages, but that such lettings cannot be excluded from the exemption in favour of the 'leasing or letting of immovable property' if they are closely linked to lettings of immovable property for another purpose which are themselves exempt from VAT.

> Article 13B(b) of the Sixth Directive must be interpreted as meaning that Member States may not exempt from value-added tax lettings of premises and sites for parking which are not covered by the exemption provided for in that provision, that is to say, those which are not closely linked to lettings of immovable property for another purpose which are themselves exempt from VAT.

C-63/92   *Lubbock Fine & Co. Commissioners of Customs and Excise*

> The term 'letting of immovable property' used in Article 13B(b) of the Sixth Directive to define an exempt transaction covers the case where a tenant surrenders his lease and returns the immovable property to his immediate landlord.

> Article 13B(b) of the Sixth Directive, which allows Member States to apply further exclusions to the scope of the exemption for the letting of immovable property, does not authorize them to tax the consideration paid by one party to the other in connection with the surrender of the lease when the rent paid under the lease was exempt from VAT.

C-346/95   *Elisabeth Blasi v Finanzamt Munchen I*

> Article 13B(b)(1) of the Sixth Directive may be constructed as meaning that what is defined in German law as the provision of short-term accommodation for guests constitutes, within the meaning of Community law, the provision of accommodation in sectors with a function similar to that of the hotel sector, thus being subject to VAT.

> It is compatible with Article 13B(b)(1) of the Sixth Directive to draw a distinction between taxable transactions and exempt transactions on the basis of the duration of the accommodation, such exemption being reserved for those letting transactions that involve the conclusion of a letting agreement for more than six months.

C-60/96   *Commission of the European Communities v French Republic*

> By introducing and maintaining in force an administrative provision extending to the letting of certain forms of movable property the exemption from VAT, which pursuant Article 13B(b) of the Sixth Directive is restricted exclusively to the letting of immovable property, France failed to fulfil its obligations under Article 2 of that Directive.

C-381/97   *Belgocodex SA v Belgian State*

Article 2 of the First Directive does not preclude a Member State which has availed itself of the possibility provided for by Article 13C of the Sixth Directive, and thus given its taxpayers the right to opt for taxation of certain lettings of immovable property, from abolishing, in a subsequent law, that right of option and thus reintroducing the exemption in full.

C-12/98   *Miguel Amengual v Amengual Far*

Article 13B(b) of the Sixth Directive allows Member States, by general rule, to subject to VAT lettings of immovable property and, by way of exception, to exempt only lettings of immovable property to be used for dwelling purposes.

C-409/98   *Mirror Group plc v Commissioners of Customs and Excise*

Article 13B(b) of the Sixth Directive must be interpreted as not exempting from VAT a supply made by a person who does not initially have any interest in the immovable property, where that person enters into an option agreement in relation to leases of that immovable property in return for a sum of money being paid to the person, on terms that the money will remain in a special account as security for its obligations under the option agreement.

Article 13B(b) of the Sixth Directive should be interpreted as not exempting from VAT a supply made by a person who does not initially have any interest in the immovable property, where that person subsequently exercises the option under the option agreement and accepts the grant of the immovable property in return for the release of the money in the special account to the person.

C-108/99   *Commissioners of Customs and Excise v Cantor Fitzgerald International*

Article 13B(b) of the Sixth Directive must be interpreted as not exempting from VAT a supply made by a person who does not have any interest in immovable property, where the person agrees to accept an assignment of a lease of that immovable property from a lessee, and the lessee pays that person a sum of money in return for that person taking the assignment of the lease in that immovable property.

C-150/99   *Stockholm Lindopark AB v Svenska Staten (Swedish State)*

Articles 13A(1)(m) and 13B(b) of the Sixth Directive preclude national legislation from providing for a general exemption from VAT for the supply of premises and other facilities and the related supply of accessories or other arrangements for the practice of sport or physical education, including services supplied by profit-making organisations.

The implementation of a general exemption from VAT for the supply of premises and other facilities and the related supply of accessories or other arrangements for the practice of sport or physical education, where no such general exemption is to be found in the Sixth Directive, constitutes a serious breach of Community law that can render a Member State liable in damages.

C-326/99   *Stichting 'Goed Wonen' v Staatssecretaris van Financien*

Article 13B(b) and C(a) do not preclude adoption of a national provision which for the purposes of applying the VAT exemption allow the grant of a usufructuary right over immovable property for a limited period of time to be regarded as leasing or letting of immovable property.

C-269/00   *Wolfgang Seeling v Finanzamt Starnberg*

Articles 6(2)(a) and 13B(b) of the Sixth Directive, must be interpreted as precluding national legislation which treats as an exempt supply of services, on the basis that it constitutes a leasing or letting of immovable property within the meaning of Article 13B(b), the private use by a taxable person of part of a building which is treated as forming, in its entirety, part of the assets of his business.

C-315/00   *Rudolf Maierhofer v Finanzamt Augsburg-Land*

The letting of a building constructed from prefabricated components fixed to or in the ground in such a way that they cannot be easily dismantled or easily moved constitutes a letting of immovable property for the purposes of Article 13B(b) of Sixth Directive, even if the building is to be removed at the end of the lease and re-used on another site.

Whether the lessor makes available to the lessee both the building and the land on which it is erected or merely the building which he has erected on the lessee's land is irrelevant in determining whether a letting constitutes a letting of immovable property for the purposes of Article 13B(b) of the Sixth Directive.

C-275/01   *Commissioners of Customs and Excise v Sinclair Collis Limited*

On a proper construction of Article 13B(b) of the Sixth Directive, the grant, by the owner of premises to an owner of a cigarette vending machine, of the right to install the machine, and to operate and maintain it in the premises for a period of two years, in a place nominated by the owner of the premises, in return for a percentage of the gross profits on the sales of cigarettes and other tobacco goods in the premises, but with no rights of possession or control being granted to the owner of the machine other than those expressly set out in the agreement between the parties, does not amount to a letting of immovable property within the meaning of that provision.

C-428/02   *Fonden Marselisborg Lystbådehavn v Skatteministeriet*

1. Article 13B(b) of Sixth Council Directive must be interpreted as meaning that the concept of letting of immovable property includes the letting of both water-based mooring berths for pleasure boats and land sites for storage of boats on port land.

2. Article 13B(b)(2) of Sixth Directive must be interpreted as meaning that the definition of 'vehicles' includes boats.

C-269/03 *Grand Duchy of Luxembourg and Administration de l'enregistrement et des domains v Vermietungsgesellschaft Objekt Kirchberg SARL*

The provisions of subparagraph (a) of the first paragraph and of the second paragraph of Article 13(C) of Sixth Council Directive do not preclude a Member State, which has exercised the power to allow taxpayers a right of option for taxation on leasing or letting transactions of immovable property, from adopting legislation which makes full deduction of the input VAT paid conditional upon non-retroactive, prior approval of the tax authorities.

C-284/03 *Belgian State v Temco Europe SA*

Article 13B(b) of Sixth Council Directive must be interpreted as meaning that transactions by which one company, through a number of contracts, simultaneously grants associated companies a licence to occupy a single property in return for a payment set essentially on the basis of the area occupied and by which the contracts, as performed, have as their essential object the making available, in a passive manner, of premises or parts of buildings in return for a payment linked to the passage of time, are transactions comprising the 'letting of immovable property' within the meaning of that provision and not the provision of a service capable of being categorised in a different way.

Supply of goods used wholly for the purpose of exempted activities (paragraph B(c))

C-45/95 *Commission of the European Communities v Italian Republic*

By enacting and maintaining in force legislation which does not exempt from VAT supplies of goods used wholly for an exempted activity or otherwise excluded from the right to deduct, Italy failed to fulfil its obligations under Article 13B(c) of the Sixth Directive.

Financial services (paragraph B(d))

Case 8/81 *Ursula Becker v Finanzamt Münster-Innenstadt*

As from 1 January 1979, it was possible for the provision concerning the exemption from turnover tax of transactions consisting of the negotiation of credit contained in Article 13B(d)(1) of the Sixth Directive to be relied upon, in the absence of the implementation of that directive, by a credit negotiator where he had refrained from passing that tax on to persons following him in the chain of supply, and the State could not claim, as against him, that it had failed to implement the directive.

Case 255/81 *R.A. Grendel GmbH v Finanzamt fur Korperschaften, Hamburg*

As from 1 January 1979, it was possible for the provision concerning the exemption from turnover tax of transactions consisting of the negotiation of credit contained in Article 13B(d)(1) of the Sixth Directive to be relied upon, in the absence of the implementation of that directive, by a credit negotiator where he had refrained from passing that tax on to persons following him in the chain of supply, and the State could not claim, as against him, that it had failed to implement the directive.

Case 70/83   *Gerda Kloppenburg v Finanzamt Leer*

In the absence of the implementation of the Sixth Directive, it was possible for the provision concerning the exemption of the negotiation of credit contained in Article 13B(d)(1) of that directive to be relied upon by a credit negotiator in relation to transactions carried out between 1 January and 30 June 1978 where he had refrained from passing that tax on to persons following him in the chain of supply.

Case 207/87   *Gerd Weissgerber v Finanzamt Neustadt/Weinstrasse*

In the absence of implementation of the Sixth Directive, a credit negotiator may rely on the tax exemption provision contained in Article 13B(d)(1) of the directive in respect of transactions carried out between 1 January and 30 June 1978 and as from 1 January 1979 if he did not pass that tax on to the person receiving his services so as to entitle that person to deduct the input tax.

C-281/91   *Muys' en De Winter's Bouw-en Aannemingsbedrijf BV v Staatssecretaris van Financien*

Article 13(B)(d)(1) of the Sixth Directive, must be interpreted as meaning that a supplier of goods or services who authorizes his customer to defer payment of the price, in return for payment of interest, is in principle making an exempt grant of credit within the meaning of that provision. However, where a supplier of goods or services grants his customer deferral of payment of the price, in return for payment of interest, only until delivery, that interest does not constitute consideration for the grant of credit but part of the consideration obtained for the supply of goods or services within the meaning of Article 11(A)(1)(a) of the Sixth Directive.

C-2/95   *Sparekassernes Datacenter (SDC) v Skatteministeriet*

Points 3 and 5 of Article 13B(d) of the Sixth Directive, are to be interpreted as meaning that the exemption is not subject to the condition that the transactions be effected by a certain type of institution, by a certain type of legal person or wholly or partly by certain electronic means or manually.

The exemption provided for by points 3 and 5 of Article 13B(d) of the Sixth Directive is not subject to the condition that the service be provided by an institution which has a legal relationship with the end customer. The fact that a transaction covered by those provisions is effected by a third party but appears to the end customer to be a service provided by the bank does not preclude exemption for the transaction.

Point 3 of Article 13B(d) of the Sixth Directive is to be interpreted as meaning that transactions concerning transfers and payments and transactions in shares, interests in companies or associations, debentures and other securities include transactions carried out by a data-handling centre if those transactions are distinct in character and are specific to, and essential for, the exempt transactions.

Services consisting in making financial information available to banks and other users are not covered by points 3 and 5 of Article 13B(d) of the Sixth Directive.

The mere fact that transactions concerning the management of deposits, purchase contracts and loans are carried out by a data-handling centre does not prevent them from constituting services covered by points 13 and 15 of Annex F to the Sixth Directive. It is for the national court to determine whether, before 1 January 1991, those transactions were separate in character and specific to, and essential for, those services.

The mere fact that a service is invoiced by a third party does not prevent the transaction to which it relates from being exempt under points 3 and 5 of Article 13B(d) of the Sixth Directive.

C-16/00   *Cibo Participations SA v Directeur régional des impôts du Nord-Pas-de-Calais*

The involvement of a holding company in the management of companies where it entails the supply of administrative, financial, commercial and technical services constitutes an economic activity.

The expenditure incurred by a holding company, in respect of services purchased in connection with the acquisition of a shareholding in a subsidiary, forms part of its general costs.

The proportion of VAT expenditure of a holding company attributable to transactions in respect of which VAT is deductible, is deductible.

The receipt of dividends does not fall within the scope of VAT.

C-235/00   *Commissioners of Customs and Excise v CSC Financial Services Limited (formerly Continuum (Europe) Limited)*

The provision of call centre services to financial institutions, which constitute preliminary stages of the issue and transfer of securities, are not regarded as exempt services under Article 13B(d)(5) of the Sixth Directive.

C-77/01   *Empresa de Desenvolvimento Mineiro SGPS SA (EDM) v Fazenda Pública*

1) In a situation such as that in the main proceedings:

activities which consist in the simple sale of shares and other securities, such as holdings in investment funds, do not constitute economic activities within the meaning of Article 4(2) of Sixth Directive and therefore do not come within the scope of that directive;

placements in investment funds do not constitute supplies of services 'effected for consideration' within the meaning of Article 2(1) of Sixth Directive and therefore likewise do not come within the scope thereof;

the amount of turnover relating to those transactions must consequently be excluded from the calculation of the deductible proportion referred to in Articles 17 and 19 of that directive;

by contrast the annual granting by a holding company of interest-bearing loans to companies in which it has a shareholding and placements by that holding company in bank deposits or in securities, such as Treasury notes or certificates of deposit, constitute economic activities carried out by a taxable person acting as such within the meaning of Articles 2(1) and 4(2) of Sixth Directive;

however, the said transactions are exempted from value added tax under points 1 and 5 of Article 13B(d) of that directive;

in calculating the deductible proportion referred to in Articles 17 and 19 of Sixth Directive, those transactions are to be regarded as incidental transactions within the meaning of the second sentence of Article 19(2) thereof in so far as they involve only very limited use of assets or services subject to value added tax; although the scale of the income generated by financial transactions within the scope of Sixth Directive may be an indication that those transactions should not be regarded as incidental within the meaning of that provision, the fact that income greater than that produced by the activity stated by the undertaking concerned to be its main activity is generated by such transactions does not suffice to preclude their classification as 'incidental transactions';

it is for the national court to establish whether the transactions concerned in the main proceedings involve only very limited use of assets or services subject to value added tax and, if so, to exclude interest generated by those transactions from the denominator of the fraction used to calculate the deductible proportion.

C-305/01   *Finanzamt Gross-Gerau v MKG-Kraftfahrzeuge-Factoring GmbH*

An economic activity by which a business purchases debts, assuming the risk of the debtors' default, and, in return, invoices its clients in respect of commission, constitutes debt collection and factoring within the meaning of the final clause of Article 13B(d)(3) of the Sixth Directive and is therefore excluded from the exemption laid down by that provision.

Gambling (paragraph B(f))

C-283/95   *Fischer, Karlheinz v Finanzamt Donaueschingen*

Article 13B(f) should be interpreted as meaning that a Member State may not impose VAT on the unlawful operation of a *roulette* when the corresponding activity carried on by a licensed public casino is exempted.

C-453/02   *Finanzamt Gladbeck v Edith Linneweber*

1. Article 13B(f) of Sixth Council Directive precludes national legislation which provides that the operation of all games of chance and

gaming machines is exempt from VAT where it is carried out in licensed public casinos, while the operation of the same activity by traders other than those running casinos does not enjoy that exemption.

2. Article 13B(f) of the Sixth Directive has direct effect in the sense that it can be relied on by an operator of games of chance or gaming machines before national courts to prevent the application of rules of national law which are inconsistent with that provision.

Supply of building (paragraph B(g))

Case 73/85   *Hans-Dieter and Ute Kerrut v Finanzamt Monchengladbach-Mitte*

The supply of goods and services under a parcel of contracts for work and services in connection with the construction of a building, except the supply of the building land, must not be regarded as exempt under Article 13B(g) of the Sixth Directive.

Supply of land (paragraph B(h))

C-468/93   *Gemeente Emmen v Belastingdienst Grote Ondernemingen*

It is for the Member States to define the concept of 'building land' within the meaning of the combined provisions of Article 13B(h) and Article 4(3)(b) of the Sixth Directive. It therefore does not fall to the Court to specify what degree of improvement land which has not been built on must exhibit in order to be categorized as building land within the meaning of that directive.

Article 14

Exemptions on importation

1. Without prejudice to other Community provisions, Member States shall exempt the following under conditions which they shall lay down for the purpose of ensuring the correct and straightforward application of such exemption and of preventing any possible evasion, avoidance or abuse:

   (a) final importation of goods of which the supply by a taxable person would in all circumstances be exempted within the country;

   (b) ...

   (c) ...

   (d) final importation of goods qualifying for exemption from customs duties other than as provided for in the Common Customs Tariff. However, Member States shall have the option of not granting exemption where this would be liable to have a serious effect on conditions of competition;

   This exemption shall also apply to the import of goods, within the meaning of Article 7(1)(b), which would be capable of benefiting from the exemption set out above if they had been imported within the meaning of Article 7(1)(a).

   (e) reimportation by the person who exported them of goods in the state in which they were exported, where they qualify for exemption from customs duties;

   (f) ...

   (g) importation of goods:

   – under diplomatic and consular arrangements, which qualify for exemption from customs duties,

   – by international organizations recognized as such by the public authorities of the host country, and by members of such organizations, within the limits and under the conditions laid down by the international conventions establishing the organizations or by headquarters agreements,

   – into the territory of Member States which are parties to the North Atlantic Treaty by the armed forces of other States which are parties to that Treaty for the use of such forces or the civilian staff accompanying them or for supplying their messes or canteens where such forces take part in the common defence effort:

(h) importation into ports by sea fishing undertakings of their catches, unpro-cessed or after undergoing preservation for marketing but before being supplied;

(i) the supply of services, in connection with the importation of goods where the value of such services is included in the taxable amount in accordance with Article 11B(3)(b);

(j) importation of gold by Central Banks.

(k) import of gas through the natural gas distribution system, or of electricity.

2. The Commission shall submit to the Council at the earliest opportunity propos-als designed to lay down Community tax rules clarifying the scope of the exemp-tions referred to in paragraph 1 and detailed rules for their implementation.

Until the entry into force of these rules, Member States may:

– maintain their national provisions in force on matters related to the above provisions,

– adapt their national provisions to minimize distortion of competition and in particular the non-imposition or double imposition of value added tax within the Community,

– use whatever administrative procedures they consider most appropriate to achieve exemption.

Member States shall inform the Commission, which shall inform the other Member States, of the measures they have adopted and are adopting pursuant to the preceding provisions.

Notes

Amendments

– Subparagraph (1)(k) inserted by Article 1(3) of **Council Directive 2003/92/EC of 7 October 2003** [I.A.2.b.(22).].

– Article 1(8) of **Council Directive 92/111/EEC of 14 December 1992** [I.A.2.b.(6).] introduced the following amendments:

  – subparagraph (c) was deleted;

  – subparagraph (d) was amended.

– Article 1(11) of **Council Directive 91/680/EEC of 16 December 1991** [I.A.2.b.(4).] introduced the following amendments:

  – subparagraphs (b) and (f) were deleted;

  – subparagraph (c) was replaced;

– subparagraphs (d) and (g) were amended.

Amendments in preparation

– Article 399 of Proposal for a Council Directive on the common system of value added tax (Recast) – **COM(2004) 246 final, 15 April 2004** [I.C.2.a.(6).].

Derogations in force

Denmark

– By way of derogation from paragraph 1(d), **Council Decision 2005/258/EC of 14 March 2005** [I.A.2.c.Denmark(4).] authorised Denmark to apply VAT on the importation into Denmark of magazines, periodicals or the like, printed in the territory of the Community, as defined in Article 3 of the said Directive and sent to private individuals in Denmark.

Germany

– By way of derogation to subparagraph 1(g), Article 1 of **Council Decision 90/640/EEC of 3 December 1990** [I.A.2.c.Germany(4).] authorised Germany to exempt, with refund of the tax paid certain imports of the Soviet armed forces and supplies of goods and services to those same forces.

Ancillary legislation

– **Council Directive 83/181/EEC of 28 March 1983** determining the scope of Article 14(1)(d) of Directive 77/388/EEC as regards exemption from value added tax on the final importation of certain goods [I.A.2.d.(1).(a).].

Ancillary legislation no longer in force

– **Council Directive 83/183/EEC of 28 March 1983** on tax exemptions applicable to permanent imports from a Member State of the personal property of individuals [I.B.2.c.(2).(a).].

– **Council Directive 83/182/EEC of 28 March 1983** on tax exemptions within the Community for certain means of transport temporarily imported into one Member State from another [I.B.2.c.(1).].

Connected legislation no longer in force

– Article 10 and Annex A(16), (17), (18) and (19) of the **Second Council Directive 67/228/EEC of 11 April 1967** [I.B.1.].

Connected legislation in preparation

– Articles 128, 137, 140 and 141 of Proposal for a Council Directive on the common system of value added tax (Recast) – **COM(2004) 246 final, 15 April 2004** [I.C.2.a.(6).].

EU VAT cases

Free samples (paragraph 1(a))

Case 257/86   *Commission of the European Communities v Italian Republic*

Declares that by adopting and maintaining in force legislation which does not grant exemption from VAT to all imports of free samples of low value and lacks clarity and precision with regard to the exemption of certain imports of such samples, while providing for exemption for similar samples produced domestically, Italy failed to fulfil its obli-gations under Article 95 of the Treaty and Article 14(1)(a) of the Sixth Directive.

Motor vehicles (paragraph 1(c))

Case 823/79   *Criminal proceedings against Giovanni Carciati*

The rules of the EEC treaty relating to the free movement of goods do not preclude the imposition by national rules on persons residing in the territory of a Member State of a prohibition, subject to criminal penalties, on the use of motor vehicles admitted under temporary importation arrangements and thus exempt from payment of VAT.

Case 249/84   *Ministere public and Ministry of Finance v Venceslas Profant*

Article 14(1)(c) of the Sixth Directive precludes the levying by a Member State of VAT on the importation of a motor vehicle purchased in another Member State, where VAT was paid and the vehicle is registered, when the vehicle is used by a national of the second Member State resident in that state but studying in the first Member State, where for the period of his studies his name is entered in the aliens' register. Whether or not the person in question is married is irrelevant.

Case 127/86   *Ministere public and Ministre de Finances du royanne de Belgique v Yves Ledoux*

Article 14(1)(c) of the Sixth Directive prevents a Member State from levying VAT on a motor vehicle which is owned by an employer established in another Member State where VAT has been paid, and which is used by a frontier worker residing in the first Member State for the performance of his duties under his contract of employment and, secondarily, for leisure purposes.

Article 15

Exemption of exports from the Community and like transactions and international transport

Without prejudice to other Community provisions Member States shall exempt the following under conditions which they shall lay down for the purpose of ensuring the correct and straightforward application of such exemptions and of preventing any evasion, avoidance or abuse:

1. The supply of goods dispatched or transported to a destination outside the Community by or on behalf of the vendor;

2. The supply of goods dispatched or transported to a destination outside the Community by or on behalf of a purchaser not established within the territory of the country, with the exception of goods transported by the purchaser himself for the equipping, fuelling and provisioning of pleasure boats and private aircraft or any other means of transport for private use;

In the case of the supply of goods to be carried in the personal luggage of travellers, this exemption shall apply on condition that:

– the traveller is not established within the Community,

– the goods are transported to a destination outside the Community before the end of the third month following that in which the supply is effected,

– the total value of the supply, including value added tax, is more than the equivalent in national currency of ECU 175, fixed in accordance with Article 7(2) of Directive 69/169/EEC; however, Member States may exempt a supply with a total value of less than the amount.

For the purposes of applying the second subparagraph:

– a traveller not established within the Community shall be taken to mean a traveller whose domicile or habitual residence is not situated within the Community. For the purposes of this provision, 'domicile or habitual residence' shall mean the place entered as such in a passport, identity card or other identity documents which the Member State within whose territory the supply takes place recognises as valid,

– proof of exportation shall be furnished by means of the invoice or other document in lieu thereof, endorsed by the customs office where the goods left the Community.

Each Member State shall transmit to the Commission specimens of the stamps it uses for the endorsement referred to in the second indent of the third subparagraph. The Commission shall transmit this information to the tax authorities in the other Member States.

3. The supply of services consisting of work on movable property acquired or imported for the purpose of undergoing such work within the territory of the Community, and dispatched or transported out of the Community by the person providing the services or by his customer who is not established within the territory of the country or on behalf of either of them;

4. The supply of goods for the fuelling and provisioning of vessels:

    (a) used for navigation on the high seas and carrying passengers for reward or used for the purpose of commercial, industrial or fishing activities;

    (b) used for rescue or assistance at sea, or for inshore fishing, with the exception, for the latter, of ships' provisions;

    (c) of war, as defined in subheading 89.01 A of the Common Customs Tariff, leaving the country and bound for foreign ports or anchorages.

    The Commission shall submit to the Council as soon as possible proposals to establish Community fiscal rules specifying the scope of and practical arrangements for implementing this exemption and the exemptions provided for in (5) to (9). Until these rules come into force, Member States may limit the extent of the exemption provided for in this paragraph.

5. The supply, modification, repair, maintenance, chartering and hiring of the sea-going vessels referred to in paragraph 4(a) and (b) and the supply, hiring, repair and maintenance of equipment – including fishing equipment – incorporated or used therein;

6. The supply, modification, repair, maintenance, chartering and hiring of aircraft used by airlines operating for reward chiefly on international routes, and the supply, hiring, repair and maintenance of equipment incorporated or used therein;

7. The supply of goods for the fuelling and provisioning of aircraft referred to in paragraph 6;

8. The supply of services other than those referred to in paragraph 5, to meet the direct needs of the sea-going vessels referred to in that paragraph or of their cargoes;

9. The supply of services other than those referred to in paragraph 6, to meet the direct needs of aircraft referred to in that paragraph or of their cargoes;

10. Supplies of goods and services:

    – under diplomatic and consular arrangements,

    – to international organizations recognized as such by the public authorities of the host country, and to members of such organizations, within the limits and under the conditions laid down by the international conventions establishing the organizations or by headquarters agreements,

– effected within a Member State which is a party to the North Atlantic Treaty and intended either for the use of the forces of other States which are parties to that Treaty or of the civilian staff accompanying them, or for supplying their messes or canteens when such forces take part in the common defence effort.

– to another Member State and intended for the forces of any Member State which is a party to the North Atlantic Treaty, other than the Member State of destination itself, for the use of those forces or of the civilian staff accompanying them, or for supplying their messes or canteens when such forces take part in the common defence force.

This exemption shall be subject to limitations laid down by the host Member States until Community tax rules are adopted.

In cases where the goods are not dispatched or transported out of the country, and in the case of services, the benefit of the exemption may be given by means of a refund of the tax.

11. Supplies of gold to Central Banks;

12. Goods supplied to approved bodies which export them from the Community as part of their humanitarian, charitable or teaching activities outside the Community. This exemption may be implemented by means of a refund of the tax;

13. The supply of services including transport and ancillary transactions, but excluding the supply of services exempted in accordance with Article 13, when these are directly connected with the export of goods or to the imports of goods covered by the provisions of Articles 7(3) or Article 16(1), Title A;

14. Services supplied by brokers and other intermediaries, acting in the name and for account of another person, where they form part of transactions specified in this Article, or of transactions carried out outside the Community.

This exemption does not apply to travel agents who supply in the name and for account of the traveller services which are supplied in other Member States.

15. The Portuguese Republic may treat sea and air transport between the islands making up the autonomous regions of the Azores and Madeira and between those regions and the mainland in the same way as international transport.

Notes

Amendments

- The second and third subparagraphs of paragraph 2 were substituted by Article 1(3) of **Council Directive 95/7/EC of 10 April 1995** [I.A.2.b.(10).].

- Article 1(9) of **Council Directive 92/111/EEC of 14 December 1992** [I.A.2.b.(6).] introduced the following amendments:

  - the second and third subparagraphs of paragraph 2 were inserted;

  - paragraphs 3 and 10 were amended;

  - the second subparagraph of paragraph 4 and paragraph 13 were substituted.

- Article 1(12) to (19) of **Council Directive 91/680/EEC of 16 December 1991** [I.A.2.b.(4).] introduced the following amendments:

  - the heading and paragraphs 3 and 13 were substituted;

  - paragraphs 1, 2, 10, 12 and 14 were amended;

  - the last indent of paragraph 10 was inserted.

- Paragraph 15 was inserted by Article 26, Annex I, Part V, Point 2 of the **Act of Accession 1985–Portugal and Spain** (*OJ L302, 15/11/1985, p. 0167*).

Amendments in preparation

- Article 399 of Proposal for a Council Directive on the common system of value added tax (Recast) – **COM(2004) 246 final, 15 April 2004** [I.C.2.a.(6).].

- Proposal for a Council Directive amending Directive 77/388/EEC as regards Value Added Tax on services provided in the postal sector – **COM(2003) 234 final of 5 May 2003 and COM(2004) 468 final, 8 July 2004** [I.C.2.a.(3).].

Derogations in force

Germany

- By way of derogation to paragraph 10, Article 1 of **Council Decision 90/640/EEC of 3 December 1990** [I.A.2.c.Germany(4).] authorised Germany to exempt, with refund of the tax paid certain imports of the Soviet armed forces and supplies of goods and services to those same forces.

Ancillary legislation in preparation

- Proposal for a Council Regulation laying down implementing measures for Directive 77/388/EEC on the common system of value added tax – **COM(2004)641 final/2, 25 October 2004** [I.C.2.c.(3)].

Connected legislation no longer in force

- Article 10 and Annex A(16), (17), (18) and (19) of the **Second Council Directive 67/228/EEC of 11 April 1967** [I.B.1.].

Connected legislation in preparation

– Articles 128, 142, 143, 144, 145, 147, 148 and 149 of Proposal for a Council Directive on the common system of value added tax (Recast) – **COM(2004) 246 final, 15 April 2004** [I.C.2.a.(6).].

EU VAT cases

Supply of goods to a destination outside the Community by vendor (paragraph 1)

C-111/92 *Wilfried L ange v Finanzamt Furstenfeldbruck*

Article 15(1) of the Sixth Directive is to be interpreted as meaning that the exemption for exports provided for therein may not be refused where such exports are made in breach of national provisions requiring prior authorization for exports to States for which, as a result of national provisions imposing an embargo, no authorization could have been issued in any of the Member States of the European Communities.

Vessels (paragraphs 4 and 8)

Case 168/84 *Gunter Berkholz v Finanzamt Hamburg-Mitte-Altstadt*

Article 15(8) of the Sixth Directive must be interpreted as meaning that the exemption for which it provides does not apply to the operation of gaming machines installed on board the sea-going vessels referred to in that Article.

C-185/89 *Staatssecretaris van Financien v Velker International Oil Company Ltd NV*

Article 15(4) of the Sixth Directive must be construed to the effect that only supplies to a vessel operator of goods to be used by that operator for fuelling and provisioning are to be regarded as supplies of goods for the fuelling and provisioning of vessels, but there is no requirement that the goods should be actually loaded on board the vessels at the time of their supply to the operator.

Aircrafts (paragraphs 6, 7 and 9)

C-382/02 *Cimber Air A/S v Skatteministeriet*

1. Article 15(6), (7) and (9) of the Sixth Council Directive must be interpreted as meaning that the supplies of goods and services referred to in those provisions to aircraft which operate on domestic routes but are used by airlines chiefly operating for reward on international routes are exempt from VAT.

2. It is for the national courts to assess the extent of the international business and the extent of the non-international business of such companies. In doing so, they may take account of all information which indicates the relative importance of the type of operations concerned, in particular turnover.

Article 16

Special exemptions linked to international goods traffic

1. Without prejudice to other Community tax provisions, Member States may, subject to the consultations provided for in Article 29, take special measures designed to exempt all or some of the following transactions, provided that they are not aimed at final use and/or consumption and that the amount of value added tax due on cessation of the arrangements on situations referred to at A to E corresponds to the amount of tax which would have been due had each of these transactions been taxed within the territory of the country:

A. importation of goods which are intended to be placed under warehousing arrangements other than customs;

B. supplies of goods which are intended to be:

   (a) produced to customs and, where applicable, placed in temporary storage;

   (b) placed under free zone or in a free warehouse;

   (c) placed under customs warehousing arrangements or inward processing arrangements;

   (d) admitted into territorial waters:

   – inorder to be incorporated into drilling or production platforms, for purposes of the construction, repair, maintenance, alteration or fitting-out of such platforms, or to link such drilling or production platforms to the mainland,

   – for the fuelling and provisioning of drilling or production platforms;

   (e) placed, within the territory of the country, under warehousing arrangements other than customs warehousing.

For the purposes of this Article, warehouses other than customs warehouses shall be taken to be:

– for products subject to excise duty, the places defined as tax warehousing for the purposes of Article 4(b) of Directive 92/12/EEC,

– for goods other than those subject to excise duty, the places defined as such by the Member States. However, Member States may provide for such arrangements other than customs warehousing where the goods in question are intended to be supplied at the retail stage.

Nevertheless, Member States may provide for such arrangements for goods intended for:

- taxable persons for the purposes of supplies effect under the conditions laid down in Article 28k;

- tax-free shops within the meaning of Article 28k, for the purposes of supplies to travellers taking flights or sea crossing to third countries, where those supplies are exempt pursuant to Article 15;

- taxable persons for the purposes of supplies to travellers on board air-craft or vessels during a flight or sea crossing where the place of arrival is situated outside the Community;

- taxable persons for the purposes of supplies effected free of tax pursuant to Article 15, point 10.

The places referred to in (a), (b), (c) and (d) shall be as defined by the Community customs provisions in force.

C. supplies of services relating to the supplies of goods referred to in B;

D. supplies of goods and of services carried out

- in the places listed in B(a), (b), (c) and (d) and still subject to one of the situations specified therein;

- in the places listed B(e) and still subject, within the territory of the country, to the situation specified therein.

Where they exercise the option provided for in (a) for transactions effected in customs warehouses Member States shall be take the measures necessary to ensure that they have defined warehousing arrangements other than customs warehousing which permit the provisions in (b) to be applied to the same transactions concerning goods listed in Annex J which are effected in such warehouses other than customs warehouses;

E. supplies:

- of goods referred to in Article 7(1)(a) still subject to arrangements for temporary importation with total exemption from import duty or to external transit arrangements,

- of goods referred to in Article 7(1)(b) still subject to the internal Community transit procedure provided for in Article 33a,

as well as supplies of services relating to such supplies.

By way of derogation from the first subparagraph of Article 21(1)(a), the person liable to pay the tax due in accordance with the first subparagraph shall be the person who causes the goods to cease to be covered by the arrangements or situations listed in this paragraph.

A Handbook of EU VAT Legislation
Suppl. 1 (July 2005)

When the removal of goods from the arrangements or situations referred to in this paragraph gives rise to importation within the meaning of Article 7(3), the Member State of import shall take the measures necessary to avoid double taxation within the country.

1. (a) Where they exercise the option provided for in paragraph 1, Member States shall take the measures necessary to ensure that intra-Community acquisitions of goods intended to be placed under one of the arrangements or in one of the situations referred to in paragraph 1(B) benefit from the same provisions as supplies of goods effected within the country under the same conditions.

2. Subject to the consultation provided for in Article 29, Member States may opt to exempt intra-Community acquisitions of goods made by a taxable person and imports for and supplies of goods to a taxable person intending to export them outside the Community as they are or after processing, as well as supplies of services linked with his export business, up to a maximum equal to the value of his exports during the preceding 12 months.

   When they take up this option the Member States shall, subject to the consultation provided for in Article 29, extend the benefit of this exemption to intra-Community acquisitions of goods by a taxable person, imports for and supplies of goods to a taxable person indenting to supply them, as they are or after processing, under the conditions laid down in Article 28c(A) during the preceding twelve months.

   Member States may set a common maximum amount for transactions which they exempt under the first and second subparagraphs.

3. The Commission shall submit to the Council at the earliest opportunity proposals concerning common arrangements for applying value added tax to the transactions referred to in paragraphs 1 and 2.

Notes

Amendments

– Paragraphs 1 and 1a were substituted by Article 28c(E)(1) (of this Directive), as amended by Article 1(9) of **Council Directive 95/7/EC of 10 April 1995** [I.A.2.b.(10).].

– Article 28c(E)(1) (of this Directive), as amended by Article 1(13) of **Council Directive 92/111/EEC of 14 December 1992** [I.A.2.b.(6).], introduced the following amendments:

  – paragraph 1a was inserted;

  – paragraph 2 is amended;

  – the second and third subparagraphs were inserted.

– Article 1(20) of **Council Directive 91/680/EEC of 16 December 1991** [I.A.2.b.(4).] introduced the following amendments:

   – points 1(A), (B), (C) and (D) were substituted;

   – point 1(E) is inserted.

Amendments in preparation

– Article 399 of Proposal for a Council Directive on the common system of value added tax (Recast) – **COM(2004) 246 final, 15 April 2004** [I.C.2.a.(6).].

Connected legislation no longer in force

– Article 10 and Annex A(16), (17), (18) and (19) of the **Second Council Directive 67/228/EEC of 11 April 1967** [I.B.1.].

Connected legislation in preparation

– Articles 159 and 161 of Proposal for a Council Directive on the common system of value added tax (Recast) – **COM(2004) 246 final, 15 April 2004** [I.C.2.a.(6).].

EU VAT cases

Special exemptions – General

C-305/03   *Commission of the European Communities v United Kingdom of Great Britain and Northern Ireland*

           The United Kingdom, by applying a reduced rate of value added tax to the commission paid to auctioneers on the sale by auction in the auctioneer's own name of works of art, antiques and collectors' items which have been imported under temporary importation arrangements, has failed to fulfil its obligations under Articles 2(1), 5(4)(c) and 16(1) of the Sixth Council Directive. [*Opinion of Advocate-General*]

TITLE XI – DEDUCTIONS

Article 17

Origin and scope of the right to deduct

1. The right to deduct shall arise at the time when the deductible tax becomes chargeable.

2. In so far as the goods and services are used for the purposes of his taxable transactions, the taxable person shall be entitled to deduct from the tax which he is liable to pay:

   (a) value added tax due or paid within the territory of the country in respect of goods or services supplied or to be supplied to him by another taxable person;

   (b) value added tax due or paid in respect of imported goods within the territory of the country;

   (c) value added tax due under Articles 5(7)(a), 6(3) and 28a(6);

   (d) value added tax due pursuant to Article 28a(1)(a).

3. Member States shall also grant to every taxable person the right to a deduction or refund of the value added tax referred to in paragraph 2 in so far as the goods and services are used for the purposes of:

   (a) transactions relating to the economic activities as referred to in Article 4(2) carried out in another country, which would be eligible for deduction of tax if they had been performed within the territory of the country;

   (b) transactions which are exempt pursuant to Article 14(1)(g) and (i), 15, 16(1)(B), (C), (D) or (E) or (2) or 28c(A) and (C).

   (c) any of the transactions exempted pursuant Article 13B(a) and (d)(1) to (5), when the customer is established outside the Community or when these transactions are directly linked with goods intended to be exported to a country outside the Community.

4. The refund of value added tax referred to in paragraph 3 shall be effected:

   – to taxable persons who are not established within the territory of the country but who are established in another Member State in accordance with the detailed implementing rules laid down in Directive 79/1072/EEC,

   – to taxable persons who are not established in the territory of the Community, in accordance with the detailed implementing rules laid down in Directive 86/560/EEC.

For the purposes of applying the above:

(a) the taxable persons referred to in Article 1 of Directive 79/102/EEC shall also be considered for the purposes of applying the said Directive as taxable persons who are not established in the country when, inside the territory of the country, they have only carried out supplies of goods and services to a person who has been designated as a person liable to pay the tax in accordance with Article 21(1)(a) and (c);

(b) the taxable persons referred to in Article 1 of Directive 86/560/EEC shall also be considered for the purposes of applying the said Directive as taxable persons who are not established in the Community when, inside the territory of the country, they have only carried out supplies of goods and services to a person who has been designated as the person liable to pay the tax in accordance with Article 21(1)(a);

(c) Directives 79/1072/EEC and 86/560/EEC shall not apply to supplies of goods which are, or may be, exempted under Article 28c(A) when the goods supplied are dispatched or transported by the acquirer or for his account.

5. As regards goods and services to be used by a taxable person both for transactions covered by paragraphs 2 and 3, in respect of which value added tax is deductible, and for transactions in respect of which value added tax is not deductible, only such proportion of the value added tax shall be deductible as is attributable to the former transactions.

This proportion shall be determined, in accordance with Article 19, for all the transactions carried out by the taxable person.

However, Member States may:

(a) authorize the taxable person to determine a proportion for each sector of his business, provided that separate accounts are kept for each sector;

(b) compel the taxable person to determine a proportion for each sector of his business and to keep separate accounts for each sector;

(c) authorize or compel the taxable person to make the deduction on the basis of the use of all or part of the goods and services;

(d) authorize of compel the taxable person to make the deduction in accordance with the rule laid down in the first subparagraph, in respect of all goods and services used for all transactions referred to therein;

(e) provide that where the value added tax which is not deductible by the taxable person is insignificant it shall be treated as nil.

6. Before a period of four years at the latest has elapsed from the date of entry into force of this Directive, the Council, acting unanimously on a proposal from the Commission, shall decide what expenditure shall not be eligible for

a deduction of value added tax. Value added tax shall in no circumstances be deductible on expenditure which is not strictly business expenditure, such as that on luxuries, amusements or entertainment.

Until the above rules come into force, Member States may retain all the exclusions provided for under their national laws when this Directive comes into force.

7. Subject to the consultation provided for in Article 29, each Member State may, for cyclical economic reasons, totally or partly exclude all or some capital goods or other goods from the system of deductions. To maintain identical conditions of competition, Member States may, instead of refusing deduction, tax the goods manufactured by the taxable person himself or which he has purchased in the country or imported, in such a way that the tax does not exceed the value added tax which would have been charged on the acquisition of similar goods.

Notes

Amendments

– Subparagraph 3(b) substituted by **Council Directive 2004/66/EC of 26 April 2004** [I.A.2.b.[(25).].

– Subparagraph 4(a) amended by Article 28f (of this Directive), as amended by Article 1(2) of **Council Directive 2000/65/EC of 17 October 2000** [I.A.2.b.(17).].

– Subparagraph 2(a) substituted by Article 28f (of this Directive), as amended by Article 1(10) of **Council Directive 95/7/EC of 10 April 1995** [I.A.2.b.(10).].

– Article 28f (of this Directive), as amended by Article 1(18) of **Council Directive 92/111/EEC of 14 December 1992** [I.A.2.b.(6).], introduced the following amendments:

  – subparagraph 3(b) was amended;

  – the last subparagraph of paragraph 4 was inserted.

– Paragraphs 2, 3 and 4 substituted by Article 28f (of this Directive), inserted by Article 1(22) of **Council Directive 91/680/EEC of 16 December 1991** [I.A.2.b.(4).].

– Paragraph 4 amended by Article 7 of the **Thirteenth Council Directive 86/560/EEC of 17 November 1986** [II.A.2.].

Amendments in preparation

– Proposal for a Council Directive amending Directive 77/388/EEC as regards certain measures to simplify the procedure for charging value added tax and to assist in countering tax evasion and avoidance, and repealing certain Decisions granting derogations – **COM(2005) 89 final, 16 March 2005** [I.C.2.a.(9)].

– Proposal for a Council Directive amending Directive 77/388/EEC with a view to simplifying value added tax obligations – **COM(2004) 728 final, 29 October 2004** [I.C.2.a.(8)].

- Article 399 of Proposal for a Council Directive on the common system of value added tax (Recast) – **COM(2004) 246 final, 15 April 2004** [I.C.2.a.(6).].

- Proposal for a Council Directive amending the rules governing the right to deduct Value Added Tax – **COM (98) 377(2) final of 17 June 1998** [I.C.2.a.(7).].

Derogations in force

Austria

- By way of derogation from paragraph 2, **Council Decision 2004/866/EC of 13 December 2004** [I.A.2.c.Austria(5).], authorised Austria to exclude expenditure on goods and services from the right to deduct VAT when over 90 % of the goods and services are used for the private purposes of a taxable person, or of his employees, or, more generally, for non-business purposes. This authorisation is valid until 31 December 2009.

Denmark

- By way of derogation to paragraphs 2, 3 and 4, Article 1 of **Council Decision 2000/91/EC of 24 January 2000** [I.A.2.c.Denmark(3).] authorised Denmark to apply an alternative procedure for the recovery of VAT on tolls paid for the use of the Oresund fixed link between the two countries. Although, this authorisation was initially only valid until 31 December 2002, **Council Decision 2003/65/EC of 21 January 2003** (*OJ L 25, 30/01/2003, p. 0040–0041*) extended it until 31 December 2006.

Germany

- By way of derogation from paragraph 2, **Council Decision 2004/817/EC of 19 November 2004** [I.A.2.c.Germany(19).], authorised Germany to exclude expenditure on goods and services from the right to deduct VAT when the goods and services in question are used more than 90 % for the private purposes of a taxable person or of his employees, or, more generally, for non-business purposes. This authorisation is valid until 31 December 2009.

Sweden

- By way of derogation to paragraphs 2, 3 and 4, Article 1 of **Council Decision 2000/91/EC of 24 January 2000** [I.A.2.c.Sweden(1).] authorised Sweden to apply an alternative procedure for the recovery of VAT on tolls paid for the use of the Oresund fixed link between the two countries. Although, this authorisation was initially only valid until 31 December 2002, **Council Decision 2003/65/EC of 21 January 2003** (*OJ L25, 30/01/2003, p. 0040–0041*) extended it until 31 December 2006.

United Kingdom

- By way of derogation to paragraphs 2 and 3, Article 1 of **Council Decision 98/198/EC of 9 March 1998** [I.A.2.c.United Kingdom(8).] authorised the United Kingdom to restrict to 50% the right of the hirer or lessee of a car to deduct the VAT on the cost of hiring or leasing that car where it is used for private purposes. Although, under Article 3 of this Council Decision, the authorisation was only valid until 31 December 1998, **Council Decision 2000/747/EC of 27 November 2000** (*OJ L302, 01/12/2000, p. 0063-0063*), **Council Decision 2003/909/EC of 22 December 2003** (*OJ L342, 30/12/2003, p. 0043-0044*) and **Council Decision 2004/855/EC of 7 December 2004**

(*OJ L369, 16/12/2004, p. 0061-0062*) extended this authorisation until 31 December 2003, 31 December 2004 and 31 December 2007, respectively.

– By way of derogation to paragraph 1, Article 1 of **Council Decision 97/375/EC of 9 June 1997** [I.A.2.c.United Kingdom(6).] authorised the United Kingdom to provide an optional scheme, that enterprises with an annual turnover not higher than £400,000 must postpone the right of deduction of tax until it has paid to the supplier. This authorisation was amended by Article 1 of **Council Decision 00/435/EC of 29 June 2000** (*OJ L172, 12/07/2000, p. 0024–0025*), which substituted the value '£400,000' for 'GBP 600,000' and extended the authorisation until 31 December 2003. **Council Decision 2003/909/EC of 22 December 2003** (*OJ L342, 30/12/2003, p. 0043–0044*) amended this authorisation further, substituting the value for "GBP 660, 000" and extending this authorisation until 31 December 2006.

– By way of derogation to this Article, Article 1 of **Council Decision 86/356/EEC of 21 July 1986** [I.A.2.c.United Kingdom(2).] authorised the United Kingdom to fix on a flat-rate basis the proportion of value added tax relating to expenditure on fuel used for private purposes in company cars.

Derogations no longer in force

Belgium

– By way of derogation to paragraph 4, **Council Decision 93/555/EEC of 25 October 1993** [I.B.2.b.Belgium(1).] authorised Belgium to exempt from VAT certain supplies of services where these services were rendered to taxable persons not established in the territory of the country. This authorisation was applicable until 31 December 1994. As it was not extended it ceased to have effect on that date.

Denmark

– By way of derogation to paragraph 4, **Council Decision 93/556/EEC of 25 October 1993** [I.B.2.b.Denmark(1).] authorised Denmark to exempt from VAT certain supplies of services where these services were rendered to taxable persons not established in the territory of the country. This authorisation was applicable until 31 December 1994. As it was not extended it ceased to have effect on that date.

France

– By way of derogation to paragraph 4, **Council Decision 93/557/EEC of 25 October 1993** [I.B.2.b.France(7).] authorised France to exempt from VAT certain supplies of services where these services were rendered to taxable persons not established in the territory of the country. This authorisation was applicable until 31 December 1994. As it was not extended it ceased to have effect on that date.

– By way of derogation to paragraph 2, **Council Decision 93/109/EEC of 15 February 1993** [I.B.2.b.France(6).] authorised France to exclude expenditure in respect of goods and services in cases, where private use of those goods and services accounts for more than 90% of their total use. This authorisation was applicable until 31 December 1996. As it was not extended it, thus ceased to have effect on that date.

– By way of derogation to paragraph 2, Article 1 of **Council Decision 89/488/EEC of 28 July 1989** [I.B.2.b.France(3).] authorised France to exclude expenditure in respect of goods and services in cases, where private use of those goods and services accounts for more than 90% of their total use. Under Article 2 the authorisation was only valid until 31 December 1992.

- By way of derogation to paragraph (6), Article 1 of **Council Decision 89/487/EEC of 28 July 1989** [I.B.2.b.France(2).] authorised France to exclude expenditure in respect of accommodation, food, hospitality and entertainment from the right to deduct. This Decision was declared invalid by the European Court in the case of *Ampafrance SA v Directeur des Services Fiscaux de Maine-et-Loire* (C-177/99).

Germany

- By way of derogation to paragraph 2, Article 1 of **Council Decision 2003/354/EC of 13 May 2003** [I.B.2.b.Germany(4).] authorised Germany to exclude from the right to deduct the VAT charged on expenditure on goods and services where these goods and services are used more than 90% for private purposes of a taxable person or of his employees, or more generally, for non-business purposes. This authorisation was only valid until 30 June 2004. As it was not extended it ceased to have effect on that date.

- By way of derogation to paragraph 2, Article 1 of **Council Decision 2000/186/EC of 28 February 2000** [I.B.2.b.Germany(3).] authorised Germany to exclude from the right to deduct the VAT charged on expenditure on goods and services where more than 90% of those goods and services are used for non-business purposes, and to limit to 50% the right to deduct VAT charged on expenditure on vehicles not used exclusively for business purposes. This authorisation was only valid until 31 December 2002. It was partially substituted by **Council Decision 2003/354/EC of 13 May 2003** [I.A.2.c.Germany(17).].

- By way of derogation to paragraph 4, **Council Decision 94/8/EC of 22 December 1993** [I.B.2.b.Germany(1).] authorised Germany to exempt from VAT certain supplies of services where these services were rendered to taxable persons not established in the territory of the country. This authorisation was applicable until 31 December 1994. As it was not extended it ceased to have effect on that date.

Ireland

- By way of derogation to paragraph 4, **Council Decision 93/558/EEC of 25 October 1993** [I.B.2.b.Ireland(1).] authorised Ireland to exempt from VAT certain supplies of services where these services were rendered to taxable persons not established in the territory of the country. This authorisation was applicable until 31 December 1994. As it was not extended it ceased to have effect on that date.

Italy

- By way of derogation to paragraph 4, **Council Decision 93/559/EEC of 25 October 1993** [I.B.2.b.Italy(1).] authorised Italy to exempt from VAT certain supplies of services where these services were rendered to taxable persons not established in the territory of the country. This authorisation was applicable until 31 December 1994. As it was not extended it ceased to have effect on that date.

Luxembourg

- By way of derogation to paragraph 4, **Council Decision 93/560/EEC of 25 October 1993** [I.B.2.b.Luxembourg(1).] authorised Luxembourg to exempt from VAT certain supplies of services where these services were rendered to taxable persons not established in the territory of the country. This authorisation was applicable until 31 December 1994. As it was not extended it ceased to have effect on that date.

The Netherlands

– By way of derogation to paragraph 4, **Council Decision 93/561/EEC of 25 October 1993** [I.B.2.b.The Netherlands(2).] authorised the Netherlands to exempt from VAT certain supplies of services where these services were rendered to taxable persons not established in the territory of the country. This authorisation was applicable until 31 December 1994. As it was not extended it ceased to have effect on that date.

Portugal

– By way of derogation to paragraph 4, **Council Decision 93/562/EEC of 25 October 1993** [I.B.2.b.Portugal(1).] authorised Portugal to exempt from VAT certain supplies of services where these services were rendered to taxable persons not established in the territory of the country. This authorisation was applicable until 31 December 1994. As it was not extended it ceased to have effect on that date.

Spain

– By way of derogation to paragraph 4, **Council Decision 94/501/EC of 27 July 1994** [I.B.2.b.Spain(1).] authorised Spain to exempt from VAT certain supplies of services where these services were rendered to taxable persons not established in the territory of the country. This authorisation was applicable until 31 December 1994. As it was not extended it ceased to have effect on that date.

United Kingdom

– By way of derogation to paragraphs 2 and 3, Article 1 of **Council Decision 95/252/EC of 29 June 1995** [I.B.2.b.United Kingdom(7).] authorised the United Kingdom to restrict to 50% the right of the hirer and lessee to deduct input tax on charges for the hire or lease of a passenger car where the car is used for private purposes. Under Article 3 the authorisation was only valid until 31 December 1997. This authorisation was not extended and, therefore, ceased to have effect on this date.

– By way of derogation to paragraph 4, **Council Decision 93/563/EEC of 25 October 1993** [I.B.2.b.United Kingdom(6).] authorised the United Kingdom to exempt from VAT certain supplies of services where these services were rendered to taxable persons not established in the territory of the country. This authorisation was applicable until 31 December 1994. As it was not extended it ceased to have effect on that date.

– By way of derogation to paragraph 1, Article 1 of **Council Decision 93/111/EEC of 15 February 1993** [I.B.2.b.United Kingdom(5).] authorised the United Kingdom to provide, within an optional scheme, that enterprises with an annual turnover of less than £350 000 must postpone the right of deduction of tax until it has been paid to the supplier. Under Article 1 this authorisation was only valid until 31 December 1996. As it was not extended, it ceased to have effect on this date.

– By way of derogation to paragraph 1, Article 1 of **Council Decision 90/497/EEC of 24 December 1990** [I.B.2.b.United Kingdom(3).] authorised the United Kingdom to grant undertakings with an annual turnover of less than £300 000 the option of deferring deduction of tax until it is paid to the supplier. Under Article 1 this authorisation was only valid until 31 December 1992. As it was not extended, it ceased to have effect on this date.

– By way of derogation to paragraph 1, Article 1 of **Council Decision 87/400/EEC of 23 July 1987** [I.B.2.b.United Kingdom(2).] authorised the United Kingdom to provide within an optional scheme that enterprises with an annual turnover of less than 340 000 Ecus, must postpone the right of deduction of tax until it has been paid to the supplier. Under Article 1 this authorisation was only valid until 30 September 1990. As it was not extended, it ceased to have effect on this date.

Connected legislation no longer in force

– Article 11 and Annex A(20), (21), (22) (23) and (24) of the **Second Council Directive 67/228/EEC of 11 April 1967** [I.B.1.].

Connected legislation in preparation

– Articles 162, 167, 170 and 171 of Proposal for a Council Directive on the common system of value added tax (Recast) – **COM(2004) 246 final, 15 April 2004** [I.C.2.a.(6).].

EU VAT cases

Right to deduct – general

Case 165/86   *Leesportefeuille 'Intiem' CV v Staatssecretaris van Financiën*

> Where an employer, who is a taxable person for the purposes of the rules on VAT, by agreement with one of his employees and another taxable person, the supplier, arranges for the latter to supply goods at the employer's expense to the employee, who uses them exclusively for the purposes of the employer's business, and the employer receives from the supplier invoices for those supplies charging him VAT in respect of the goods supplied, Article 11(1)(a) of the Second Directive and Article 17(2)(a) of the Sixth Directive must be interpreted as meaning that the employer may deduct the VAT with which he is so charged from the VAT payable by him.

C-342/87   *Genius Holding BV v Staatssecretaris van Financien*

> The right to deduct provided for in the Sixth Directive, does not apply to tax which is due solely because it is mentioned on the invoice.

C-291/92   *Armbrecht Dieter v Finanzam Uelzen*

> Where a taxable person sells property part of which he had chosen at the time of acquisition not to assign to his business, only the part of the property assigned to his business is to be taken into account for the application of Article 17(2) of the said directive.

C-62/93   *BP Soupergaz Anonimos Etairia Geniki Emporiki-Viomichoniki kai Antiprossopeion v Greek State*

Articles 2, 11 and 17 of the Sixth Directive, must be interpreted as precluding national rules which make the importation of finished petroleum products subject to VAT calculated on the basis of a basic price different from that provided for in Article 11 of that directive and which, by exempting traders in the petroleum sector from the obligation to submit returns, deprive them of the right to deduct VAT charged directly on transactions relating to inputs.

The provisions of the Sixth Directive, in particular Articles 13 to 17 thereof, are to be interpreted as precluding an exemption from VAT on services in respect of the transport and storage of petroleum products that are unconnected with the transport of those products from a first destination to another named destination.

The provisions of Article 11A(1) and B(1) and (2) and of Article 17(1) and (2) of the Sixth Directive confer rights on individuals on which they may rely before a national court.

A taxable person may claim, with retroactive effect from the date on which the national legislation contrary to the Sixth Directive came into force, a refund of VAT paid without being due, by following the procedural rules laid down by the domestic legal system of the Member State concerned, provided that those rules are not less favourable than those relating to similar, domestic actions nor framed in a way such as to render virtually impossible the exercise of rights conferred by Community law.

C-4/94   *BLP Group v Commissioners of Customs and Excise*

Article 2 of the First Directive and Article 17 of the Sixth Directive, must be interpreted as meaning that, except in the cases expressly provided for by those directives, where a taxable person supplies services to another taxable person who uses them for an exempt transaction, the latter person is not entitled to deduct the input VAT paid, even if the ultimate purpose of the transaction is the carrying out of a taxable transaction.

C-98/98   *Commissioners of Customs and Excise v Midland Bank plc*

Article 2 of the First Directive and Article 17(2), (3) and (5) of the Sixth Directive must be interpreted as meaning that the existence of a direct and immediate link between a particular input transaction and a particular output transaction or transactions giving rise to entitlement to deduct is necessary before the taxable person is entitled to deduct input VAT and in order to determine the extent of such entitlement.

It is for the national court to apply the 'direct and immediate link test' to the facts of each case.

A taxable person making both transactions in respect of which VAT is deductible and transactions in respect of which it is not, may not deduct in its entirely the input VAT charged on goods and services, where such goods or services have been utilised not for the purpose of carrying out a deductible transaction but in the context of activities which are no more than the consequence of making such a transaction.

C-338/98   *Commission of the European Communities v Kingdom of the Netherlands*

By providing that an employer who is a taxable person for the purposes of VAT may deduct part of an allowance paid to an employee for business use of a private car, the Netherlands failed to fulfil its obligations under Article 17(2)(a) and 18(1)(a) of the Sixth Directive.

C-396/98   *Grundstuckgemeinschaft Schlosstrasse GbR v Finanzamt Paderborn*

Article 17 of the Sixth Directive must be interpreted as meaning that a taxable person's right to deduct VAT paid on goods and services supplied to it with a view to certain leasing operations is retained where a legislative amendment post-dating the supply of such goods or services but pre-dating the commencement of the above mentioned operations deprives that taxable person of the right to waive exemption thereof, even if the VAT was assessed subject to subsequent review.

C-408/98   *Abbey National plc v Commissioners of Customs and Excise*

In circumstances where a Member State has exercised the option in Article 5(8) of the Sixth Directive, so that the transfer of a totality of assets or part thereof is regarded as not being a supply of goods, the transferor may deduct VAT on the costs of the services acquired in order to affect the transfer.

C-150/99   *Stockholm Lindopark AB v Svenska Staten (Swedish State)*

Article 17(1) and (2) have direct effect.

C-78/00   *Commission of the European Communities v Italian Republic*

By providing that the category of taxable persons whose tax position for 1992 is in credit be belatedly issued with Government bonds instead of refunds of VAT, Italy failed to fulfil its obligations under Articles 17 and 18 of the Sixth Directive.

C-487/01   *Gemeente Leusden v Staatssecretaris van Financiën*

Articles 17 and 20(2) of the Sixth Council Directive interpreted in accordance with the principles of the protection of legitimate expectations and legal certainty do not preclude the withdrawal by a Member State of the right to opt for taxation of lettings of immovable property which results in the adjustment of deductions made in respect of the immovable property acquired as capital goods which is let pursuant to Article 20 of the Sixth Directive.

Where a Member State withdraws the right to opt for taxation of lettings of immovable property, it must take account of the legitimate expectation of its taxable persons when determining the arrangements for implementing the legislative amendment. The repeal of legislation from which a taxable person has derived an advantage in paying less tax, without there being any abuse, cannot however, as such, breach a legitimate expectation based on Community law.

C-152/02   *Terra Baubedarf-Handel GmbH v Finanzamt Osterholz-Scharmbeck*

For the deduction referred to in Article 17(2)(a) of Sixth Council Directive the first subparagraph of Article 18(2) of the Sixth Directive must be interpreted as meaning that the right to deduct must be exercised in respect of the tax period in which the two conditions required by that provision are satisfied, namely that the goods have been delivered or the services performed and that the taxable person holds the invoice or the document which, under the criteria determined by the Member State in question, may be considered to serve as an invoice.

C-376/02   *Stichting 'Goed Wonen' v Staatssecretaris van Financiën*

Where a taxable person has, under Article 17 of Sixth Council Directive, acquired without abuse or fraud an entitlement to deduct the VAT paid on immovable property which has been transferred to him and which, whilst originally intended for letting (a transaction not subject to tax) has subsequently been granted in usufruct (a transaction subject to tax) without there having been any subsequent change in the planned use of the said property, the principles of legal certainty and protection of legitimate expectation preclude an adjustment of the tax not deducted, as mentioned in Article 20(1)(a) of that directive, from being revoked on the sole ground that, following a legislative amendment which had not yet taken place at the time of the grant of the usufruct, that transaction is regarded with retroactive effect as an exempt transaction not giving rise to any deduction entitlement. [*Opinion of Advocate-General*]

C-25/03   *Finanzamt Bergisch Gladbach v HE*

A taxable person who purchases a property in co-ownership with his spouse and uses it in part for the purposes of his own independent business is entitled, under Article 17(2)(a) of the Sixth Directive, to deduct from the VAT for which he is liable the proportion of the VAT paid for the purchase of the part of the property used for business purposes which corresponds to his share of ownership. [*Opinion of Advocate-General*]

C-465/03   *Kretztechnik AG v Finanzamt Linz*

In becoming listed on a stock market and in issuing shares in that connection to new shareholders in return for the issue price, a public limited company does not make a supply for consideration within the meaning of Article 2(1) of the Sixth Directive.

Input tax on services acquired for the purposes of such a share issue may be deducted to the extent that the company charges VAT on its output transactions, in accordance with Article 17(1), (2) and (5) of the Sixth Directive. [*Opinion of Advocate-General*]

Right to deduct – preparatory activities (paragraph 1 and 2)

C-37/95   *Belgium v Ghent Coal Terminal NV*

Article 17 of the Sixth Directive must be constructed as allowing a taxable person acting as such to deduct the VAT payable by him on goods or services supplied to him for the purpose of investment work intended to be used in connection with taxable transactions. The right to deduct remains acquired where, by reason of circumstances beyond his control, the taxable person has never made use of those goods or services for the purpose of carrying out taxable transactions.

C-110/98   *Galbafrisa SL and Others v Agencia Estatal de Administracion Tributaria (AEAT)*

Article 17 of the Sixth Directive precludes national legislation which makes the exercise of the right to deduct VAT paid by a taxable person liable thereto before he starts regularly carrying out taxable transactions conditional upon the fulfilment of certain requirements, and which penalises infringement of those requirements by forfeiture of the right to deduct or deferment of the exercise of that right until the time at which taxable transactions actually begin to be carried out on a regular basis.

C-400/98   *Finanzamt Goslar v Brigitte Breitsohl*

Articles 4 and 17 of the Sixth Directive are to be interpreted as meaning that the right to deduct the VAT paid on the transactions carried out with a view to the realisation of a planned economic activity still exists even where the tax authority is aware, from the time of the first assessment, that the economic activity envisaged, which was to give rise to taxable transactions, will not be taken up.

Limitation of right to deduct (paragraph 2)

Case 50/87   *Commission of the European Communities v French Republic*

By introducing and maintaining in force, in breach of the Sixth Directive, fiscal rules which, for undertakings that let immovable property which they have acquired or had built, limit the right to deduct value-added tax paid on inputs where the amount of the proceeds of the letting of such immovable property is less than one-fifteenth of its value, France failed to fulfil its obligations under the Treaty.

C-97/90   *Lennartz v Finanzamt Muchen III*

A taxable person who uses goods for the purposes of an economic activity has the right on the acquisition of those goods to deduct input tax in accordance with the rules laid down in Article 17 of the Sixth Directive, however small the proportion of business use. A rule or administrative practice imposing a general restriction on the right of deduction in cases where there is limited, but none the less genuine, business use constitutes a derogation from Article 17 of the directive and is valid only if the requirements of Article 27(1) or Article 27(5) of the directive are met.

C-43/96   *Commission of the European Communities v French Republic*

By maintaining in force legislation which denies taxable persons the right to deduct VAT on means of transport which constitute the very tool of their trade, France did not fail to fulfil its obligations under Article 17(2) and (6) of the Sixth Directive.

C-345/99   *Commission of the European Communities v French Republic*

By applying to vehicles used by taxable persons carrying on the activity of driving instructions the condition that, in order to be able to deduct VAT charged on the initial acquisition of those vehicles, they must be used exclusively for that activity, France failed to fulfil its obligations under Article 17(2) of the Sixth Directive.

C-40/00   *Commission of the European Communities v French Republic*

By reintroducing, after the date of entry into force of the Sixth Directive, a total prohibition on the right to deduct VAT on diesel used as fuel for vehicles on the purchase of which no VAT is deductible, France failed to fulfil its obligations under Article 17(2) of the Sixth Directive.

C-17/01   *Finanzamt Sullingen v Walter Sudholz*

1) Consideration of the procedure prior to the adoption of Council Decision 2000/186/EC of 28 February 2000 has disclosed no irregularity such as to affect the validity of that decision.

2) Article 3 of Decision 2000/186/EC is invalid in that it provides for the authorisation granted by the Council to the Federal Republic of Germany to have retroactive effect from 1 April 1999.

3) Article 2 of Decision 2000/186/EC meets the substantive requirements of Article 27(1) of the Sixth Directive and is not invalid.

C-33/03   *Commission of the European Communities v United Kingdom of Great Britain and Northern Ireland*

By granting taxable persons the right to deduct value added tax on certain supplies of fuel to non-taxable persons, contrary to the provisions of Articles 17(2)(a) and 18(1)(a) of Sixth Council Directive, the United Kingdom of Great Britain and Northern Ireland has failed to fulfil its obligations under that directive.

C-204/03   *Commission of the European Communities v Kingdom of Spain*

By limiting the right to deduct value added tax in the conditions defined by Articles 102(1) and 104(2) of Law No 37/1992 of 28 December 1992 on value added tax as amended by Law No 66/1997 of 30 December 1997, the Kingdom of Spain has failed to fulfil its obligations under Articles 17 and 19 of the Sixth Council Directive [*Opinion of Advocate-General*]

C-243/03   *Commission of the European Communities v French Republic*

En instaurant une règle particulière limitant la déductibilité de la taxe sur la valeur ajoutée afférente à l'achat de biens d'équipement en raison du fait qu'ils ont été financés au moyen de subventions, la République française a manqué aux obligations qui lui incombent en vertu du droit communautaire et, notamment, des articles 17 et 19 de la sixième directive [*Opinion of Advocate-General*]

Apportionment of tax (paragraph 5)

C-98/98   *Commissioners of Customs and Excise v Midland Bank plc*

Article 2 of the First Directive and Article 17(2), (3) and (5) of the Sixth Directive must be interpreted as meaning that the existence of a direct and immediate link between a particular input transaction and a particular output transaction or transactions giving rise to entitlement to deduct is necessary before the taxable person is entitled to deduct input VAT and in order to determine the extent of such entitlement.

It is for the national court to apply the 'direct and immediate link test' to the facts of each case.

A taxable person making both transactions in respect of which VAT is deductible and transactions in respect of which it is not, may not deduct in its entirely the input VAT charged on goods and services, where such goods or services have been utilised not for the purpose of carrying out a deductible transaction but in the context of activities which are no more than the consequence of making such a transaction.

C-408/98   *Abbey National plc v Commissioners of Customs and Excise*

In circumstances where a Member State has exercised the option in Article 5(8) of the Sixth Directive, so that the transfer of a totality of assets or part thereof is regarded as not being a supply of goods, the transferor may deduct VAT on the costs of the services acquired in order to affect the transfer.

C-16/00   *Cibo Participations SA v Directeur régional des impôts du Nord-Pas-de-Calais*

The expenditure incurred by a holding company, in respect of services purchased in connection with the acquisition of a shareholding in a subsidiary, forms part of its general costs.

The proportion of VAT expenditure of a holding company attributable to transactions in respect of which VAT is deductible, is deductible.

The receipt of dividends does not fall within the scope of VAT.

C-465/03   *Kretztechnik AG v Finanzamt Linz*

In becoming listed on a stock market and in issuing shares in that connection to new shareholders in return for the issue price, a public limited company does not make a supply for consideration within the meaning of Article 2(1) of the Sixth Directive.

Input tax on services acquired for the purposes of such a share issue may be deducted to the extent that the company charges VAT on its output transactions, in accordance with Article 17(1), (2) and (5) of the Sixth Directive. [*Opinion of Advocate-General*]

Standstill clause (paragraph 6)

C-43/96   *Commission of the European Communities v French Republic*

By maintaining in force legislation which denies taxable persons the right to deduct VAT on means of transport which constitute the very tool of their trade, France did not fail to fulfil its obligations under Article 17(2) and (6) of the Sixth Directive.

C-305/97   *Royscot Leasing Ltd and others v Commissioners of Customs and Excise*

Article 11(4) of the Second Directive authorised Member States to introduce or retain, and Article 17(6) of the Sixth Directive authorises them to retain, general exclusions from the right to deduct the VAT payable on the purchase of motor cars used by a taxable person for the purposes of his taxable transactions.

On a proper construction of Article 17(6) of the Sixth Directive, Member States may retain the exclusions from the right to deduct VAT referred to in its second subparagraph, even though the Council did not decide, before the expiry of the period laid down in the first subparagraph, which expenditure should not be eligible for deduction of VAT.

C-177/99   *Ampafrance SA v Directeur des Services Fiscaux de Maine-et-Loire*

Council Decision 89/487/EEC of 28 July 1989 authorising France to apply a measure derogating from the second paragraph of Article 17(6) of the Sixth Directive is invalid.

C-409/99   *Metropol Treuhand WirtschaftstreuhandgmbH v Finanzlandesdirektion fur Steiermark*

The second paragraph of Article 17(6) of the Sixth Directive must be interpreted as precluding a Member State from excluding, after the entry into force of the Sixth Directive, expenditure relating to certain motor vehicles from the right to deduct VAT where, at the date of entry into force of that Directive, that expenditure gave rise to the right to deduct VAT in accordance with a consistent practice of the public authorities of that State on the basis of a ministerial circular.

The first sentence of Article 17(7) of the Sixth Directive must be interpreted as not authorising a Member State to exclude goods from the system of VAT deductions,

(a) without first consulting the VAT Committee provided for in Article 29 of the Sixth Directive;

(b) without limitation in time, in order to consolidate its budget.

C-40/00   *Commission of the European Communities v French Republic*

By reintroducing, after the date of entry into force of the Sixth Directive, a total prohibition on the right to deduct VAT on diesel used as fuel for vehicles on the purchase of which no VAT is deductible, France failed to fulfil its obligations under Article 17(2) of the Sixth Directive.

C-155/01   *Cookies World Vertriebsgesellschaft mbH iL v Finanzlandesdirektion für Tirol*

The provisions of the Sixth Council Directive preclude a measure of a Member State which provides that payment for services supplied in other Member States to a person in the first Member State is subject to VAT whereas, had the services in question been supplied within the territory of the country, the person to whom they were supplied would not have been entitled to deduction of input tax.

C-434/03   *P. Charles and T.S. Charles-Tijmens v Staatssecretaris van Financiën*

National legislation, in existence when the Sixth Directive came into force, which provides for a general exclusion from the right of deduction in respect of all goods and services used for non-business purposes does not come within the scope of the second subparagraph of Article 17(6) of that directive. [*Opinion of Advocate-General*]

Exclusion of goods from the system of deductions (paragraph 7)

C-409/99   *Metropol Treuhand WirtschaftstreuhandgmbH v Finanzlandesdirektion fur Steiermark*

The second paragraph of Article 17(6) of the Sixth Directive must be interpreted as precluding a Member State from excluding, after the entry into force of the Sixth Directive, expenditure relating to certain motor vehicles from the right to deduct VAT where, at the date of entry into force of that Directive, that expenditure gave rise to the right to deduct VAT in accordance with a consistent practice of the public authorities of that State on the basis of a ministerial circular.

The first sentence of Article 17(7) of the Sixth Directive must be interpreted as not authorising a Member State to exclude goods from the system of VAT deductions,

(a) without first consulting the VAT Committee provided for in Article 29 of the Sixth Directive;

(b) without limitation in time, in order to consolidate its budget.

C-155/01   *Cookies World Vertriebsgesellschaft mbH iL v Finanzlandesdirektion für Tirol*

The provisions of the Sixth Council Directive preclude a measure of a Member State which provides that payment for services supplied in other Member States to a person in the first Member State is subject to VAT whereas, had the services in question been supplied within the territory of the country, the person to whom they were supplied would not have been entitled to deduction of input tax.